Betjeman's
Cornwall

John Betjeman first fell in love with Cornwall during his childhood holidays and he has been returning to it yearly ever since. As this collection shows, it has inspired some of his best poems and most evocative prose. Many other places in Britain and Ireland—urban, suburban, and rural—have been celebrated by him, but the Cornish cliffs and beaches, modest churches and formidable sea have the power to stir him which only first love possesses.

Opening with two long passages from his verse autobiography *Summoned by Bells*, this collection then alternates between poems and prose, interspersed with many old photographs, some more recent ones by John Gay, Edwin Smith and others, and specially commissioned drawings by John Piper. The text of John Betjeman's television programme 'One Man's County' (1964) is also included for the first time.

John Betjeman owes much to Cornwall, but the Delectable Duchy has been equally fortunate in its adoption by the Laureate.

Betjeman's *Cornwall*

JOHN MURRAY

Title page illustration
'The next five and a half miles beside the
broadening Camel to Padstow is the most
beautiful train journey I know'

This selection © John Betjeman 1984
The Acknowledgements on page 96
constitute an extension of this copyright page

First published 1984
by John Murray (Publishers) Ltd
50 Albemarle Street, London W1X 4BD
Reprinted 1984, 1986, 1988

Design by Ian Craig
Typeset by Fakenham Photosetting Ltd, Fakenham
Printed and bound in Great Britain
by the Camelot Press, Southampton

British Library Cataloguing in Publication Data

Betjeman, John
Betjeman's Cornwall.
I. Title
828'.91208   PR6003.E77
ISBN 0-7195-4106-9

Contents

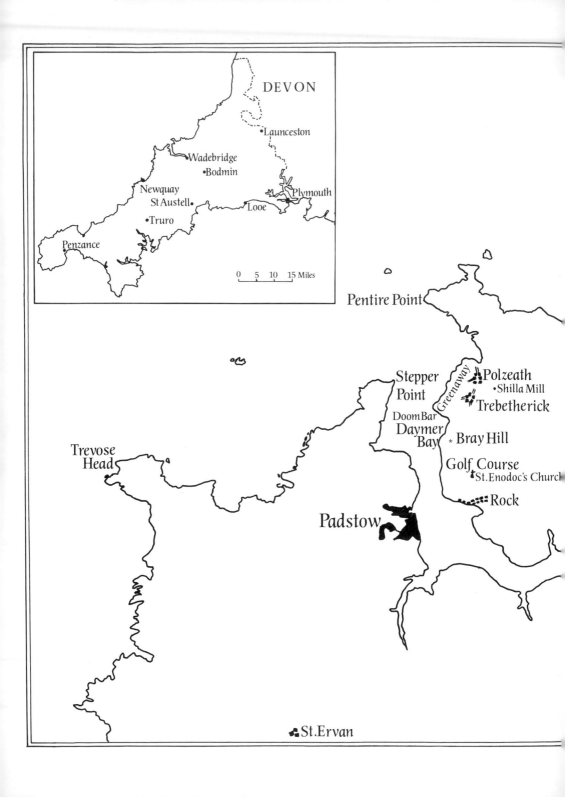

DEVON

•Launceston

•Wadebridge
•Bodmin

Newquay
St Austell•
•Truro
Looe
Plymouth

Penzance

0   5   10   15 Miles

Pentire Point

Stepper
Point

Greenaway

Polzeath
•Shilla Mill
Trebetherick

Doom Bar
Daymer
Bay
* Bray Hill

Golf Course
St.Enodoc's Church

Trevose
Head

Rock

Padstow

St.Ervan

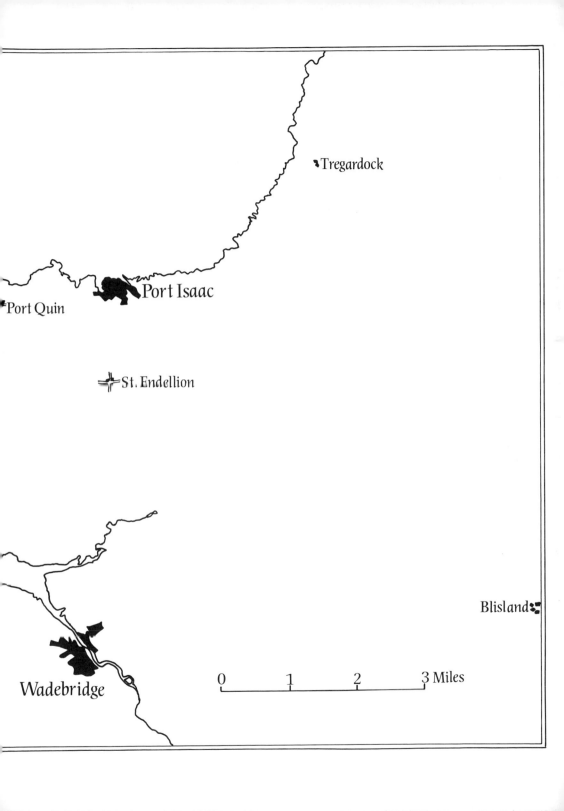

Tregardock

Port Isaac

Port Quin

St. Endellion

Blisland

Wadebridge

0   1   2   3 Miles

Summoned By Bells
from Chapters IV and VIII

Come, Hygiene, goddess of the growing boy,
I here salute thee in Sanatogen!
Anaemic girls need Virol, but for me
Be Scott's Emulsion, rusks, and Mellin's Food,
Cod-liver oil and malt, and for my neck
Wright's Coal Tar Soap, Euthymol for my teeth.
Come, friends of Hygiene, Electricity
And those young twins, Free Thought and clean Fresh Air:
Attend the long express from Waterloo
That takes us down to Cornwall. Tea-time shows
The small fields waiting, every blackthorn hedge
Straining inland before the south-west gale.
The emptying train, wind in the ventilators,
Puffs out of Egloskerry to Tresméer
Through minty meadows, under bearded trees
And hills upon whose sides the clinging farms
Hold Bible Christians. Can it really be
That this same carriage came from Waterloo?
On Wadebridge station what a breath of sea
Scented the Camel valley! Cornish air,
Soft Cornish rains, and silence after steam . . .
As out of Derry's stable came the brake
To drag us up those long, familiar hills,
Past haunted woods and oil-lit farms and on
To far Trebetherick by the sounding sea.
   Oh what a host of questions in me rose:
Were spring tides here or neap? And who was down?
Had Mr Rosevear built himself a house?
Was there another wreck upon Doom Bar?
The carriage lamps lit up the pennywort
And fennel in the hedges of the lane;

Huge slugs were crawling over slabs of slate;
Then, safe in bed, I watched the long-legg'd fly
With red transparent body tap the walls
And fizzle in the candle flame and drag
Its poisonous-looking abdomen away
To somewhere out of sight and out of mind,
While through the open window came the roar
Of full Atlantic rollers on the beach.
    Then before breakfast down toward the sea
I ran alone, monarch of miles of sand,
Its shining stretches satin-smooth and vein'd.
I felt beneath bare feet the lugworm casts
And walked where only gulls and oyster-catchers
Had stepped before me to the water's edge.
The morning tide flowed in to welcome me,
The fan-shaped scallop shells, the backs of crabs,
The bits of driftwood worn to reptile shapes,
The heaps of bladder-wrack the tide had left
(Which, lifted up, sent sandhoppers to leap
In hundreds round me) answered 'Welcome back!'
Along the links and under cold Bray Hill
Fresh water pattered from an iris marsh
And drowned the golf-balls on its stealthy way
Over the slates in which the elvers hid,
And spread across the beach. I used to stand,
A speculative water engineer—
Here I would plan a dam and there a sluice
And thus divert the stream, creating lakes,
A chain of locks descending to the sea.
Inland I saw, above the tamarisks,
From various villas morning breakfast smoke
Which warned me then of mine; so up the lane
I wandered home contented, full of plans,
Pulling a length of pink convolvulus
Whose blossoms, almost as I picked them, died.
    Bright as the morning sea those early days!
Though there were tears, and sand thrown in my eyes,

'Was there another wreck upon Doom Bar?'
The *Angèle* of Boulogne, wrecked on 13 November, 1911

And punishments and smells of mackintosh,
Long barefoot climbs to fetch the morning milk,
Terrors from hissing geese and angry shouts,
Slammed doors and waitings and a sense of dread,
Still warm as shallow sea-pools in the sun
And welcoming to me the girls and boys.

Daymer from Bray Hill

Daymer Bay in 1920

Wet rocks on which our bathing dresses dried;
Small coves, deserted in our later years
For more adventurous inlets down the coast:
Paralysis when climbing up the cliff—
Too steep to reach the top, too far to fall,
Tumbling to death in seething surf below,
A ledge just wide enough to lodge one's foot,

A sea-pink clump the only thing to clutch,
Cold wave-worn slate so mercilessly smooth
And no one near and evening coming on—
Till Ralph arrived: 'Now put your left foot here.
Give us your hand' . . . and back across the years
I swing to safety with old friends again.
Small seem they now, those once tremendous cliffs,
Diminished now those joy-enclosing bays.
    Sweet were the afternoons of treasure-hunts.
We searched in pairs and lifted after showers
The diamond-sparkling sprays of tamarisk:
Their pendent raindrops would release themselves
And soak our shirt-sleeves. Then upon the links
Under a tee-box lay a baffling clue:
A foursome puffing past the sunlit hedge
With rattling golf bags; all the singing grass
Busy with crickets and blue butterflies;
The burnet moths, the unresponsive sheep
Seemed maddeningly indifferent to our plight . . .

    Childhood is measured out by sounds and smells
And sights, before the dark of reason grows.
Ears! Hear again the wild sou'westers whine!
Three days on end would the September gale
Slam at our bungalows; three days on end
Rattling cheap doors and making tempers short.
It mattered not, for then enormous waves
House-high rolled thunderous on Greenaway,
Flinging up spume and shingle to the cliffs.
Unmoved amid the foam, the cormorant
Watched from its peak. In all the roar and swirl
The still and small things gained significance.
Somehow the freckled cowrie would survive
And prawns hang waiting in their watery woods;
Deep in the noise there was a core of peace;

Deep in my heart a warm security.
    Nose! Smell again the early morning smells:
Congealing bacon and my father's pipe;
The after-breakfast freshness out of doors
Where sun had dried the heavy dew and freed
Acres of thyme to scent the links and lawns;
The rotten apples on our shady path
Where blowflies settled upon squashy heaps,
Intent and gorging; at the garden gate
Reek of Solignum on the wooden fence;
Mint round the spring, and fennel in the lane,
And honeysuckle wafted from the hedge;
The Lynams' cess-pool like a body blow;
Then, clean, medicinal and cold—the sea.
'Breathe in the ozone, John. It's iodine.'
But which is iodine and which is drains?
Salt and hot sun on rubber water-wings . . .
Home to the luncheon smell of Irish stew
And washing-up stench from the kitchen sink
Because the sump is blocked. The afternoons
Brought coconut smell of gorse; at Mably's farm
Sweet scent of drying cowdung; then the moist
Exhaling of the earth in Shilla woods—
First earth encountered after days of sand.
Evening brought back the gummy smell of toys
And fishy stink of glue and Stickphast paste,
And sleep inside the laundriness of sheets.
    Eyes! See again the rock-face in the lane,
Years before tarmac and the motor-car.
Across the estuary Stepper Point
Stands, still unquarried, black against the sun;
On its Atlantic face the cliffs fall sheer.
Look down into the weed world of the lawn—
The devil's-coach-horse beetle hurries through,
Lifting its tail up as I bar the way
To further flowery jungles.
                                    See once more

The Padstow ferry, worked by oar and sail,
Her outboard engine always going wrong,
Ascend the slippery quay's up-ended slate,
The sea-weed hanging from the harbour wall.
Hot was the pavement under, as I gazed
At lanterns, brass, rope and ships' compasses
In the marine-store window on the quay.
The shoe-shop in the square was cool and dark.
The Misses Quintrell, fancy stationers,
Had most to show me—dialect tales in verse
Published in Truro (Netherton and Worth)
And model lighthouses of serpentine.
Climb the steep hill to where that belt of elm
Circles the town and church tower, reached by lanes
Whose ferny ramparts shelter toadflax flowers
And periwinkles. See hydrangeas bloom
In warm back-gardens full of fuchsia bells.
To the returning ferry soon draws near
Our own low bank of sand-dunes; then the walk
Over a mile of quicksand evening-cold.
    It all is there, excitement for the eyes,
Imagined ghosts on unfrequented roads
Gated and winding up through broom and gorse
Out of the parish, on to who knows where?
What pleasure, as the oil-lamp sparkled gold
On cut-glass tumblers and the flip of cards,
To feel protected from the night outside:
Safe Cornish holidays before the storm!

'I'm free! I'm free!' The open air was warm
And heavy with the scent of flowering mint,
And beetles waved on bending leagues of grass,
And all the baking countryside was kind.
    Dear lanes of Cornwall! With a one-inch map,
A bicycle and well-worn *Little Guide*,

Those were the years I used to ride for miles
To far-off churches. One of them that year
So worked on me that, if my life was changed,
I owe it to St Ervan and his priest
In their small hollow deep in sycamores.
The time was tea-time, calm free-wheeling time,
When from slashed tree-tops in the combe below
I heard a bell-note floating to the sun;
It gave significance to lichened stone
And large red admirals with outspread wings
Basking on buddleia. So, coasting down
In the cool shade of interlacing boughs,
I found St Ervan's partly ruined church.
Its bearded Rector, holding in one hand
A gong-stick, in the other hand a book,
Struck, while he read, a heavy-sounding bell,
Hung from an elm bough by the churchyard gate,
'Better come in. It's time for Evensong.'
     There wasn't much to see, there wasn't much
The *Little Guide* could say about the church.
Holy and small and heavily restored,
It held me for the length of Evensong,
Said rapidly among discoloured walls,
Impatient of my diffident response.
'Better come in and have a cup of tea.'
The Rectory was large, uncarpeted;
Books and oil-lamps and papers were about;
The study's pale green walls were mapped with damp;
The pitch-pine doors and window-frames were cracked;
Loose noisy tiles along the passages
Led to a waste of barely furnished rooms:
Clearly the Rector lived here all alone.
     He talked of poetry and Cornish saints;
He kept an apiary and a cow;
He asked me which church service I liked best—
I told him Evensong . . . 'And I suppose
You think religion's mostly singing hymns

16

Padstow Quay: a view towards the railway station, 1907

Padstow

And feeling warm and comfortable inside?'
And he was right: most certainly I did.
'Borrow this book and come to tea again.'
With Arthur Machen's *Secret Glory* stuffed
Into my blazer pocket, up the hill
On to St Merryn, down to Padstow Quay
In time for the last ferry back to Rock,
I bicycled—and found Trebetherick
A worldly contrast with my afternoon.
    I would not care to read that book again.
It so exactly mingled with the mood
Of those impressionable years, that now
I might be disillusioned. There were laughs
At public schools, at chapel services,
At masters who were still 'big boys at heart'—
While all the time the author's hero knew
A Secret Glory in the hills of Wales:
Caverns of light revealed the Holy Grail

Exhaling gold upon the mountain-tops;
At 'Holy! Holy! Holy!' in the Mass
King Brychan's sainted children crowded round,
And past and present were enwrapped in one.
    In quest of mystical experience
I knelt in darkness at St Enodoc;
I visited our local Holy Well,
Whereto the native Cornish still resort
For cures for whooping-cough, and drop bent pins
Into its peaty water . . . Not a sign:
No mystical experience was vouchsafed:
The maidenhair just trembled in the wind
And everything looked as it always looked . . .
But somewhere, somewhere underneath the dunes,
Somewhere among the cairns or in the caves
The Celtic saints would come to me, the ledge
Of time we walk on, like a thin cliff-path
High in the mist, would show the precipice.

One Man's County

The visitors have come to Cornwall. 'Visitors', 'foreigners' we're called by the Cornish. I'm a visitor. We litter the cliffs with our houses. We litter the cliffs with our shacks. When I was a boy, all this place was open fields. And Cornwall is older than the Cornish. Come down to the sea's edge, and watch the Atlantic and hear the words of the Cornish poet Hawker:

> They come, they mount, they charge in vain.
> Thus far, incalculable main.
> No more. Thy hosts have not o'erthrown
> The lichen on the barrier stone.
> Have the rocks faith, that thus they stand
> Unmoved, a grim and stately band?
> Have the proud billows thought on life
> To feel the glory of the strife?
> Hear how their din of madness raves,
> The battled army of the waves.
> Thy way, oh God, is in the sea,
> Thy paths, where awful waters be.
> Thy spirit thrills the conscious stone.
> Oh Lord, thy footsteps are not known.

How many million years ago, what volcanic eruptions of the earth's surface happened to twist these cliffs into those contorted shapes? The bones and undercrust of Cornwall are so old that the grass and trees and buildings on its surface seem trivial by comparison. For instance, I used to be told, I expect wrongly, when I was young that the white streaks you see in the slate were compressed oceans—fish and sand.

If you come up on to the moors, you can see what the surface of Cornwall looked like before man came to live on it. Gigantic granite boulders are strewn about the highest places. Right on the top,

Brown Willy, Bodmin Moor

they're piled on top of one another like, for example, The Cheese-ring at Liskeard. People think that man made that monument. Wrong, nature did it. Centuries of wind and rain have worn away the surrounding earth and made it smooth. When trees have dared to grow above the valleys, those same centuries of south-west winds have hammered them down and bent them inward, leaning from the sea. The Cornish moors are spotted with granite boulders, and the granite boulders are spotted with many-coloured lichens. The granite boulders moulder. They decompose and make a thin soil. Out of the soil grow primeval-looking shrubs, their branches hung with silvery beards of lichen.

To these high moors came early man to Cornwall. On view-commanding hills he built earth enclosures to protect his tribe and herds of cattle. From here he could watch out for the enemy—wild animals from thick woods below, or human enemies. The Danes and Saxons turned these camps into forts for subduing the Celtic Cornish, as here at Warpstow. Stone-age, Bronze-age, Iron-age. The Cornish moors were full of people. Their ghosts are there today—ghosts of prehistoric fields here on the Land's End peninsula. A race of giants must have built the hedges of those little enclosures. Late Bronze-age man, in about 2000 BC, first streamed the Cornish moors for tin and copper ore, and sold it to the ancient Greeks. Surface tin-streaming works survive on the moors. The Cornish moors are full of ghosts: ghosts of forgotten worship in those stone circles of the Iron-age pagans. And earlier than that, in the Stone-age, there were the quoits of Cornwall. They were the tombs of Stone-age men, and covered over once with a mound of earth. What was this early religion about? At Menontol, on the Land's End peninsula, the shapes of the stones suggest fertility worship.

Then came the Christian missionaries from Wales to Cornwall, four centuries after Christ, and carved their crosses on pagan standing stones. They blessed the wells and lived in bee-hive huts beside pools and streams. They stood waist-high in the fresh running water by their cells and recited the Psalter. St Petroc, St Endellion, St Minver, St Tudy, St Teth, St Enodoc. They floated over on mill-stones and cabbage leaves from Wales and Ireland. But really I think in coracles. They used the brown moorland water for baptising Iron-age pagans. They made Cornwall Christian, even before St Augustine brought the gospel to Kent. They were a band of holy hermits, monks and nuns of the ancient Celtic church. And about them all sorts of legends have grown.

In these gentler times, so near to Christ, men moved down from the moorland into the wooded valleys. They ground corn by water power, and they made clearings in the thick woods for farming. Where fresh water meets the sea—and it's always running to meet the sea from the high land down to the coast of Cornwall—all round the coast the Cornish settled at the sea's edge, in places where they could get away from the wind, and they fished, as here at Boscastle.

Snug, slate houses tucked into the side of the hill, looking down on to each other's roofs, looking up into each other's gardens.

The Cornish have always been a religious people. Almost every Cornish church was rebuilt in the sixteenth century on the site of the cell of the Celtic saint who'd founded it a thousand years before, and rebuilt in splendid style, of that hardest and most intractable material, granite. Look at it close, to see how it weathers. Look at it in a quarry on Bodmin moor, and see how hard it is to work, even today. Watch how they split it. That man down there is drilling holes. Then the staples are driven in and hammered, and now wait. At last! All that to get a single slab. And after this the surface has to be

St Mary Magdalene's Church, Launceston: 'the miracle of Cornish carving'

'Slate . . . the other chief building material of Cornwall . . . designed
into patterns and graded into shapes'

24

smoothed and squared. Remember all the effort when you look at the hard surface of granite. Remember how hard it is to make the slightest impression. And after you've been watching that, look at the miracle of Cornish carving. The outside walls of St Mary Magdalene's church, Launceston, carved out of moorland granite in 1511, and finished in 1524.

John Wesley inspired the Cornish in Georgian times rather as the Celtic saints had inspired them a thousand years before. What shoutings of glory must have been heard from those windows; what soul-converting sermons and full-throated Hallelujahs must have sounded from here. No Cornish settlement seems complete without its Methodist or Bible Christian chapel for the humbler people. Cornwall was never a place of really big landowners. Most of the landowners were small squires, royalists in the Civil War, or recusants like the Rosscarrocks, who lived here and suffered for their faith. They had granite and slate manor houses hidden in wooded valleys. They farmed the hills around. And many of these old Cornish manor houses have reverted to farms again. That slate piggery at Rosscarrock was built when Shakespeare was alive, and it is as good today as it was then. Slate. That's the other chief building material of Cornwall. Slate, which flakes and splits, and keeps the weather out. You see it all over the houses, pale blue and silvery when it's old, and designed into patterns and graded into shapes. Slate. You can tell where you are in Cornwall from the colour of the local slate. Nearly every parish used to have its own quarry, except in the granite districts. Now they're all disused, except Delabole there, the biggest one, which has been going on since the reign of King Stephen. Slate, the memorial headstones of Cornish churchyards are worth a film to themselves. Memorials. The fine flourishy engraved slate of Georgian headstones in Cornish churchyards are one sort.

There's another sort of memorial, and they are the granite chimney stacks and slate chimney stacks in the churchyards of the Cornish tin and copper industry. These chimneys are memorials to the Cornish engineers. Men like Trevithick and Hornblower, who in the eighteenth century improved on stationary steam engines for pumping up water out of the wet mines. Water was always the trouble with tin mining. And hauling up minerals from a thousand feet below. For all its empty open look this desolate country is dangerous to walk on. Underneath it is a honeycomb of hundreds of miles of passages in the hot granite. Some shafts go down 2000 feet. One false step and you might find yourself plunged into black, hot silence. A silence always hangs about St Day. It was once one of the chief mining towns of Cornwall. These streets were once like Oxford Street, a century and more ago, to ill-paid tin miners. After long hours in the hot wet granite passages below the earth they'd look into these shop windows, they and their poor families, gazing and gazing and longing to buy. For all its melancholy, St Day is now the least spoiled town in Cornwall.

Brunel's great railway bridge and viaduct linked Cornwall with England, and as the Great Western flourished, so did Cornwall's newer industry, derived from tin mining, the industry of china clay. The clay itself comes from decaying granite and is used for pottery, paper, face powder, dozens of things, and exported all over the world. The white silica waste, when the clay has been extracted, is lifted up on to tips and makes this lunar landscape of mountains round St Austell. Nothing will grow on these white tips. Unless there's an earthquake, those conical pyramids, seen from all over Cornwall, will continue to turn pink in the sunset and reflect the clouds. The white waste will continue to pollute brown streams, and plunge on to streak the southern estuaries with creamy mud.

It's hard to say whether the china clay industry or the tourist trade, we visitors, have done more harm to the natural beauty of Cornwall. You can't blame us for coming to Cornwall. These are Perran sands, near Newquay. We have become nomads again, like pre-historic man. St Pirran brought the gospel and built his oratory in about 800 AD, and the oratory is still there, somewhere, hidden among the dunes and shacks. Here, where St Pirran brought the gospel, we, the new nomads, bring our caravans and our signs of what we call civilisation, that's to say transistor sets and sanitation for ladies. Civilisation, or barbarism, does it much matter? When you think of the age of Cornwall and compare it with the very short time of recorded history, and the still shorter time since man has started messing about with its surface, what is it? An eternity is no time at all. It's like that boy's sandcastle. The sea wastes all.

Delabole Slate Quarry in about 1900, but 'which has been going on since the reign of King Stephen'

Old Friends

The sky widens to Cornwall. A sense of sea
   Hangs in the lichenous branches and still there's light.
The road from its tunnel of blackthorn rises free
     To a final height,

And over the west is glowing a mackerel sky
   Whose opal fleece has faded to purple pink.
In this hour of the late-lit, listening evening, why
     Do my spirits sink?

The tide is high and a sleepy Atlantic sends
   Exploring ripple on ripple down Polzeath shore,
And the gathering dark is full of the thought of friends
     I shall see no more.

Where is Anne Channel who loved this place the best,
   With her tense blue eyes and her shopping-bag falling apart,
And her racy gossip and nineteen-twenty zest,
     And that warmth of heart?

Where's Roland, easing his most unwieldy car,
   With its load of golf-clubs, backwards into the lane?
Where Kathleen Stokes with her Sealyhams? There's Doom Bar;
     Bray Hill shows plain;

For this is the turn, and the well-known trees draw near;
   On the road their pattern in moonlight fades and swells:
As the engine stops, from two miles off I hear
     St Minver bells.

What a host of stars in a wideness still and deep:
  What a host of souls, as a motor-bike whines away
And the silver snake of the estuary curls to sleep
      In Daymer Bay.

Are they one with the Celtic saints and the years between?
  Can they see the moonlit pools where ribbonweed drifts?
As I reach our hill, I am part of a sea unseen—
      The oppression lifts.

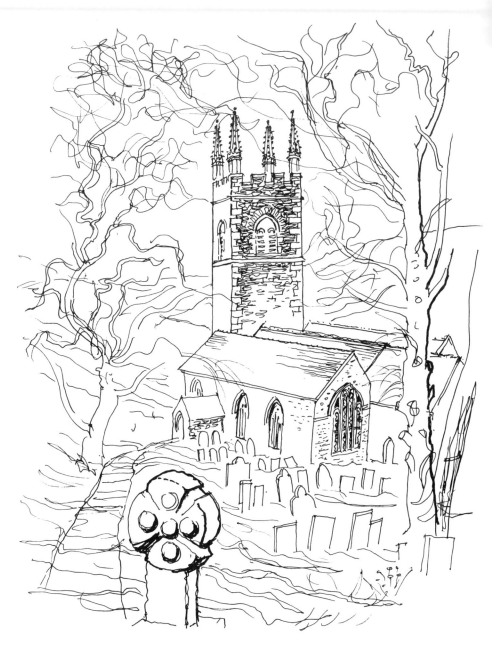

'The poet Hawker sang of the saints in Morwenstow'

Cornwall

When I first came to Cornwall over fifty years ago, as a small boy, we drove the seven miles from the station in a horse-brake; there was only one motor-car in the parish and this could not attempt the steeper hills. Roads were only partially metalled and in the lesser lanes the rock showed through on the surface. Everyone in the village had oil lamps and candles. A journey to the nearest town and back was a day's expedition. There were still many country people who had never been to London and the story used to be told of one of them who thought the metropolis was all under a glass roof because he never got further than Paddington Station. Visitors to Cornwall, 'foreigners' as they are rightly called by the Cornish, were mostly fishermen, golfers and artists. My own father, in his leisure from business in London, was all three.

The attraction of Cornish scenery for artists started with the picturesque movement at the end of the eighteenth century. Thomas Rowlandson used to stay with the Onslows at Hengar in St Tudy parish and sketch the wooded valleys of north Cornwall, the tors on Bodmin Moor, the churches, farms and cliffs. He set a fashion which other English watercolour artists and engravers followed, notably Thomas Daniell. In the 1820s Turner found inspiration in the south coast of the Duchy. By the 1880s artists were coming from England into Cornwall and settling in St Ives and Newlyn and painting not only the scenery but the people.

Some, like Stanhope Forbes, made the journey via Brittany. The first whorls of the silvery mist of the Celtic Revival had risen at Tintagel with Tennyson's *Idylls of the King*. The Cornish Celtic Revivalists, poetical and artistic, took an interest in the old Cornish language which was akin to Breton and Welsh and had died out in the eighteenth century, and in the legends of the Celtic saints. The poet Hawker sang of the saints in Morwenstow, and the indefatigable Baring-Gould told and sometimes invented picturesque legends about Celtic saints, later to be corrected by the learned Celtic hagiographer, Canon Doble. The revival of the see of Cornwall and the building of the cathedral in Truro in the eighties turned the gaze of Christians to Brittany, where the feasts of so many Cornish saints were still kept.

The romantic view of the Cornish and Cornwall has continued until the present day. The accomplished work of the Victorian artists of the Newlyn and St Ives schools is just being appreciated again, after nearly half a century's neglect. Stanhope Forbes's paintings show the Londoner's delight in the simple life, fisherfolk and the stony Celtic cottages and fields.

From the eighteenth century Opie to Peter Lanyon in the present there have, of course, been noted native artists. The Cornish themselves are not dreamy and unpractical as the 'foreigners' sometimes suppose. Like most Celts, they combine a deep sense of religion with a shrewd gift for business. These iron age people, who were Christian before the Saxons, had, until they were discovered by the tourists in the last century, a hard struggle for existence. The Saxons and the Normans tried to hold them down with forts and castles. They did not take kindly to the Reformation, nor to Cromwell, and most of them stood out for King Charles. They gained their living, since Roman times, by mining, for the minerals of Cornwall are numerous and rich, and he who buys land there likes to buy the mining rights too. They were also farmers and fishermen. Their religious faith was awakened in the eighteenth century by John Wesley and to this day the majority of the Cornish are Methodists. They had their own brand of it in the Bible Christians, a sect whose chief light was Billy Bray, the converted tin miner. Many an oil-lit chapel rang with alleluyas on a Sunday and hearts were lifted at the thought of a glorious day coming in the next life after years of ill-paid toil in the hot labyrinths of the mines. Their practical gifts came out in the invention of machinery for pumping water out of the mines and the use of steam power. They were boat-builders, craftsmen and engineers, rather than architects. For this reason the buildings of Cornwall are mostly homely and not at all grand. Only a Cornishman would have the endurance to carve intractable granite as he has done at St Mary Magdalene, Launceston, and Probus tower.

The awakening of the Cornish to the value of the tourist industry came with the railways. The Great Western extended itself into Cornwall and was thought of first in terms of goods traffic—tin, china clay and fish. The London & South-Western, the Great Western's rival, ran a line into north Cornwall via Okehampton, largely for holiday traffic. Fathers who had come for the fishing and mothers who wanted sea air for their families at cheaper rates and in less plebeian conditions than those provided in Thanet or Brighton came to Cornwall. Monster hotels were built at the beginning of this century to provide for them, such as the King Arthur's Castle at Tintagel, the Poldhu at Mullion and the Metropole at Padstow. Many a terrace of boarding houses arose in seaports which had hitherto thought that their only industry was to be fishing. Newquay and Bude are largely 'foreigners'' creations, and Falmouth, turning the corner westward of Pendennis Castle, built a new seaside town. Simultaneously with the big hotel came the early twentieth-century cult of the old cottage in the country, and picturesque ports like Polperro, St Ives, Looe and Fowey did well. Farmers' wives specialised in Cornish teas and fishermen rowed the 'foreigners' out of the harbour to catch mackerel they would otherwise be catching themselves. Farmers on the sea coast started growing bungalows instead of wheat.

All this tourist industry brought prosperity and security to Cornwall until the appearance of the Duchy was seriously altered by electricity and the motor-car. The Electricity Board has strung the fields, villages and towns of Cornwall with more poles and wires, ill-sited and clumsily arranged, than in any other part of the British Isles. This is partly because even the remotest bungalow on a cliff wants electricity and partly because burying cables in slate or granite is expensive. The motor-car has made the greatest change of all. Roads have been widened, blocks of houses have been taken down in picturesque ports to make way for car parks; petrol stations proliferate; huge hoardings to attract the motorist line the entrances to towns. In the holiday season lorries and cars trailing caravans and boats block lanes never intended for such heavy traffic. The County Planning authorities, hard put to it to find available sites on the coast, have been obliged to introduce caravans and chalets even to the wooded inland valleys. Several stretches of the coast have been rescued by the National Trust or saved, at any rate for their lifetime, by those landowners who can still afford to hold out against the blandishment of 'developers'. The old and beautiful Cornwall is now mostly to be found on foot or in a small car by those skilled in using the one-inch ordnance survey map. It is a consolation that no one yet has discovered how to build houses on the sea.

Delectable Duchy

Where yonder villa hogs the sea
Was open cliff to you and me.
The many-coloured cara's fill
The salty marsh to Shilla Mill.
And, foreground to the hanging wood,
Are toilets where the cattle stood.
The mint and meadowsweet would scent
The brambly lane by which we went;
Now, as we near the ocean roar,
A smell of deep-fry haunts the shore.
In pools beyond the reach of tides
The Senior Service carton glides,
And on the sand the surf-line lisps
With wrappings of potato crisps.
The breakers bring with merry noise
Tribute of broken plastic toys
And lichened spears of blackthorn glitter
With harvest of the August litter.
Here in the late October light
See Cornwall, a pathetic sight,
Raddled and put upon and tired
And looking somewhat over-hired,
Remembering in the autumn air
The years when she was young and fair—
Those golden and unpeopled bays,
The shadowy cliffs and sheep-worn ways,
The white unpopulated surf,
The thyme- and mushroom-scented turf,
The slate-hung farms, the oil-lit chapels,
Thin elms and lemon-coloured apples—
Going and gone beyond recall
Now she is free for 'One and All.'*
* The motto of Cornwall.

One day a tidal wave will break
Before the breakfasters awake
And sweep the cara's out to sea,
The oil, the tar, and you and me,
And leave in windy criss-cross motion
A waste of undulating ocean
With, jutting out, a second Scilly,
The isles of Roughtor and Brown Willy.

Saint Cadoc

A flame of rushlight in the cell
On holy walls and holy well
And to the west the thundering bay
With soaking seaweed, sand and spray,
   Oh good St Cadoc pray for me
   Here in your cell beside the sea.

Somewhere the tree, the yellowing oak,
Is waiting for the woodman's stroke,
Waits for the chisel saw and plane
To prime it for the earth again
   And in the earth, for me inside,
   The generous oak tree will have died.

St Cadoc blest the woods of ash
Bent landwards by the Western lash,
He loved the veinéd threshold stones
Where sun might sometime bleach his bones
    He had no cowering fear of death
    For breath of God was Cadoc's breath.

Some cavern generates the germs
To send my body to the worms,
To-day some red hands make the shell
To blow my soul away to Hell
    To-day a pair walks newly married
    Along the path where I'll be carried.

St Cadoc, when the wind was high,
Saw angels in the Cornish sky
As ocean rollers curled and poured
Their loud Hosannas to the Lord,
    His little cell was not too small
    For that great Lord who made them all.

Here where St Cadoc sheltered God
The archaeologist has trod,
Yet death is now the gentle shore
With Land upon the cliffs before
    And in his cell beside the sea
    The Celtic saint has prayed for me.

Port Isaac

Can it really be that a town is half a mile away? I have walked between high Cornish hedges from St Endellion, once the parish church of Port Isaac. The tower dwindles. The land winds. The slate of the hedges is overgrown with grasses, bed-straw and milky-pink convolvulus, pale purple scabious and here and there darker valerian. From several places standing on a hedge or looking through a gate, I can glimpse the sea. The sea is there all right, the great Atlantic, emerald green, wrinkled, glittering, sliding streaks of water, spotted dark blue here and there with reflections. It was a full tide, tamed and quiet for the moment, sliding round this inhospitable coast of North Cornwall, with white crescents of surf floating close inshore. From here on these high-up fields, where blackthorn is sliced by the sea wind and leans inland, I can see all along the rocky cliffs to Tintagel Head. Behind me is even grander coast to the Rumps Point and Pentire. Cliffs and ocean are fine to watch from these high, windy fields as cloud shadows race over them. But where can there be a town? Less than half a mile and still no sight of it!

There is no doubt this is the way to approach Port Isaac, from St Endellion on the Polzeath side of the port. The final hill is very steep and there is only a disused quarry in which you can park a motor-car if you are not on foot. Not until you round a corner do you see any sign of Port Isaac at all. Then you see it all, huddled in a steep valley, a cover at the end of a combe, roofs and roofs, tumbling down either steep hillside in a race for shelter from the south-west gales. A fresh-water stream pours brown and cold along the valley, under slate bridges, between old houses, under the road and out into the little harbour.

Port Isaac is Polperro without the self-consciousness, St Ives without the artists. The same whitewashed slate houses with feathery-looking roofs which have been 'grouted'—that is to say the old slates have been cemented over and limewashed—the same narrow airless passages between whitewashed walls. But here are winding paths that climb up steps of beautiful blue-green Delabole slate to other winding paths, hills too steep for anyone with heart trouble to manage, roads and lanes too narrow for buses or coaches. One of the sights of Port Isaac used to be to watch the Life-Boat being brought down Fore Street and missing the walls by inches as she was manoeuvred round the bend at the *Golden Lion* into the Town Platt.

Port Isaac has no grand architecture.

A simple slate Methodist chapel and Sunday school in the Georgian tradition hangs over the harbour and is the prettiest building in the town. On the opposite side of the water is a picturesque Gothic style school, from whose pointed windows the teachers could, if they wished, pitch their pupils down the cliff side into the harbour below. Then, lost in rambling cliff paths between the walls, some so narrow that a fat man could not use them, is my favourite house in Port Isaac. It is called the 'Birdcage': an irregular pentagon in shape, one small room thick, and three storeys high, and hung on the weather sides with slates which have gone a delicate silvery blue. It's empty now and obviously 'condemned'. For that is the sad thing about Port Isaac. It is the kind of place Town Planners hate: the quintessence of the quaint. There are no boulevards, no car stands or clinics. The dentist calls once a week and brings his instruments with him in his car.

The Community Centre is all wrong by Town Planning standards. It is not the public-house, but the Liberal Club. Anyone who knows Cornish fishermen must know that most of them do not drink, many are chapel-goers and a Liberal Club without a licence is the sort of place where you would expect to find them.

The trade of Port Isaac really *is* fishing. The harbour does not draw much water. It hardly is a harbour. A better description would be an unexpected cove between high cliffs. Two arms have been built out into the water to keep back the bigger seas, while great guardian headlands keep the harbour calm in most weathers. It is used by small craft and these are reached by dinghies drawn up on the Town Platt among lobster pots and nets. The promise of a dark night after a shoal of pilchards had been sighted, the sound of rowlocks and splashing of oars in harbour water, boarding the fishing boat from the dinghy, the outside roar of the sea, the dark cliffs fading in

39

Port Isaac, June 1906. The boat is the cutter *Telegraph* of Padstow

The Dolphin Inn, Port Isaac, 1906

twilight and dropping away as we move out to open sea, letting down the nets and drifting. Those were the times! Unless, like me, you were a shocking sailor and sick all night and thanking God for the dawn light and the nearing cliffs of Varley Head as you made for home and harbour.

Even if you are no sailor, the smell of fish tells you the chief business of the port. And your eyes will tell you too. For the little

42

houses (the oldest are sixteenth-century), though so huddled together and so steeply hung on to cliffs, are like all fishermen's houses, wonderfully clean and polished. Sparkling quartz, known as Cornish Diamond, is cemented into garden walls, figs and fuchsia bushes grow in tiny gardens, big shells from the Orient rest on window sills, brass and paint of front doors shine, carpentry is excellent, and all windows that *can* look out to sea, so that even as they die the old fishermen of Port Isaac may watch the tides. I expect the old people will all soon be moved to some very ugly council houses being built on the windy hilltop in those hideous grey cement things called 'Cornish blocks'.

Across stupendous cliffs, as full of flowers as a rock garden, is another little fishing port—Port Quin, an empty Port Isaac, mournful and still. For here the old cottages are nearly all ruins; the harbour is deserted, the gardens, once so trim, are grown over with elder and ash saplings, honeysuckle and fennel. The salting sheds are in ruins too. The story is that the whole fishing fleet of the village went down in a gale, and thirty-two women were left widows.

And beyond Port Quin what caves, what rocks, what shuddering heights of striped slate, what hidden beaches and barnacled boulders, what pools where seals bask, there are between here and Pentire Point. All picturesque and grand, as blazing with colour as are the strange rock pools themselves on a summer day. The colours are brighter than the tropics. The veined rock, in which the warm salt water lies, is purple with white lines and then green, then purple again. Warm forests of red seaweed grow there, and green seaweed which looks like elm trees. If there is sand on the bottom of the pool, and the red weed waving, you may see a huge prawn gliding and shooting backwards, and the sudden dash of a small fish, too quick for the eye to see more than the sudden cloud of sand it raises. Or the rock pool may be one with shells and shingle at the bottom and perhaps those rose-tinted cowries, the pearls of this coast, and a huge starfish, magnified by the water in all its pink and grey and purple colouring. Never was such colour, never is the wonder of God's creation more brought home to me than when I see the strange, merciless bright-coloured world of these Cornish rock pools. But in a storm or in a mist how infinitely horrible and mysterious this coast

43

can be, as the rollers smash and suck, the blowholes thunder, and caves syphon out fountains of sea water a hundred feet and more into the air.

> 'Tis harsh to hear from ledge or peak
> The cruel cormorants' tuneless shriek
> Fierce songs they chant, in pool or cave
> Dark wanderers of the Western wave.

So wrote Hawker the parson poet of Morwenstowe, not many miles higher up the coast. He knew that the sea is an army fighting the land, as do the men of Port Isaac. But I like to stand in summer by the bit of wall in Fore Street, and lean over to look down at the harbour and inland at the little town below me. It is evening, harvest festival time. The small Victorian church has been hung with lobster pots and dressed with crabs and seaweed—a harvest festival of the sea. Church is over, but Chapel is still on. As I stand on this view-point above the town, the seagulls are crying and wheeling, the flowery cliffs take the evening sun, the silvery slates of the old town turn pale gold. Above the lap of the harbour water, the wail of gulls and thunder of the sea beyond the headlands, comes the final hymn from the Methodist Chapel across the green and gently rolling harbour flood.

Trebetherick

We used to picnic where the thrift
  Grew deep and tufted to the edge;
We saw the yellow foam-flakes drift
  In trembling sponges on the ledge
Below us, till the wind would lift
  Them up the cliff and o'er the hedge.
Sand in the sandwiches, wasps in the tea,
Sun on our bathing-dresses heavy with the wet,
Squelch of the bladder-wrack waiting for the sea,
Fleas round the tamarisk, an early cigarette.

From where the coastguard houses stood
  One used to see, below the hill,
The lichened branches of a wood
  In summer silver-cool and still;
And there the Shade of Evil could
  Stretch out at us from Shilla Mill.
Thick with sloe and blackberry, uneven in the light,
Lonely ran the hedge, the heavy meadow was remote,
The oldest part of Cornwall was the wood as black as night,
And the pheasant and the rabbit lay torn open at the throat.

But when a storm was at its height,
  And feathery slate was black in rain,
And tamarisks were hung with light
  And golden sand was brown again,
Spring tide and blizzard would unite
  And sea came flooding up the lane.
Waves full of treasure then were roaring up the beach,
Ropes round our mackintoshes, waders warm and dry,
We waited for the wreckage to come swirling into reach,
Ralph, Vasey, Alastair, Biddy, John and I.

Then roller into roller curled
   And thundered down the rocky bay,
And we were in a water-world
   Of rain and blizzard, sea and spray,
And one against the other hurled
   We struggled round to Greenaway.
Blesséd be St Enodoc, blesséd be the wave,
Blesséd be the springy turf, we pray, pray to thee,
Ask for our children all the happy days you gave
To Ralph, Vasey, Alastair, Biddy, John and me.

Tregardock

A mist that from the moor arose
   In sea-fog wraps Port Isaac bay,
The moan of warning from Trevose
   Makes grimmer this October day.

Only the shore and cliffs are clear.
   Gigantic slithering shelves of slate
In waiting awfulness appear
   Like journalism full of hate.

On the steep path a bramble leaf
   Stands motionless and wet with dew,
The grass bends down, the bracken's brown,
   The grey-green gorse alone is new.

Cautious my sliding footsteps go
   To quarried rock and dripping cave;
The ocean, leaden still below,
   Hardly has strength to lift a wave.

I watch it crisp into its height
   And flap exhausted on the beach,
The long surf menacing and white
   Hissing as far as it can reach.

The dunlin do not move, each bird
   Is stationary on the sand
As if a spirit in it heard
   The final end of sea and land.

And I on my volcano edge
   Exposed to ridicule and hate
Still do not dare to leap the ledge
   And smash to pieces on the slate.

St Endellion

St Endellion

Saint Endellion! Saint Endellion! The name is like a ring of bells. I travelled late one summer evening to Cornwall in a motor-car. The road was growing familiar, Delabole with its slate quarry passed, then Pendogget. Gateways in the high fern-stuffed hedges showed sudden glimpses of the sea. Port Isaac Bay with its sweep of shadowy cliffs stretched all along to Tintagel. The wrinkled Atlantic Ocean had the evening light upon it. The stone and granite manor house of Tresungers with its tower and battlements was tucked away out of the wind on the slope of a valley and there on the top of the hill was the old church of St Endellion. It looked, and still looks, just like a hare. The ears are the pinnacles of the tower and the rest of the hare, the church, crouches among wind-slashed firs.

On that evening the light bells with their sweet tone were being rung for practice. There's a Ringer's rhyme in the tower, painted on a board. It shows Georgian ringers in knee breeches and underneath is written a rhyme which ends with these fine four lines:

> Let's all in love and Friendship hither come
> Whilst the shrill treble calls to thundering Tom
> And since bells are for modest recreation
> Let's rise and ring and fall to admiration.

They were ringing rounds on all six bells. But as we drew near the tower—a grand, granite, fifteenth-century tower looking across half Cornwall—as we climbed the hill the bells sounded louder even than the car. 'St Endellion! St Endellion!' they seemed to say. 'St Endellion' their music was scattered from the rough lichened openings over foxgloves, over grey slate roofs, lonely farms and feathery tamarisks, down to that cluster of whitewashed houses known as Trelights, the only village in the parish, and to Roscarrock and Trehaverock and Trefreock, heard perhaps, if the wind was right, where lanes run steep and narrow to that ruined, forgotten fishing

49

place of Port Quin, 'St Endellion!'. It was a welcome to Cornwall and in front of us the sun was setting over Gulland and making the Atlantic at Polzeath and Pentire glow like a copper shield.

Ora pro nobis Sancta Endelienta! The words are carved in strangely effective lettering on two of the new oak benches in the church. Incidentally, those carved benches, which incorporate some of the old Tudor ones, are very decent-looking for modern pews. They were designed by the present rector and carved by a local sculptress. But who was St Endellion? She was a sixth-century Celtic saint, daughter of a Welsh king, who with her sisters Minver and Teath and many other holy relations came to North Cornwall with the Gospel.

There was an Elizabethan writer who lived in the parish, Nicholas Roscarrock. He loved the old religion and was imprisoned in the Tower and put on the rack and then imprisoned again. He wrote the life of his parish saint. 'St Endelient' he called her and said she lived only on the milk of a cow:

> which cowe the lord of Trenteny kild as she strayed into his grounds; and as olde people speaking by tradition, doe report, she had a great man to her godfather, which they also say was King Arthure, whoe took the killing of the cowe in such sort, as he killed or caus'd the Man to be slaine, whom she miraculously revived.

Nicholas Roscarrock also wrote a hymn in her praise:

> To emitate in part thy vertues rare
> Thy Faith, Hope, Charitie, thy humble mynde,
> Thy chasteness, meekness, and thy dyet spare
> And that which in this Worlde is hard to finde
> The love which thou to enemye didst showe
> Reviving him who sought thy overthrowe.

When she was dying Endelient asked her friends to lay her dead body on a sledge and to bury her where certain young Scots bullocks or calves of a year old should of their own accord draw her. This they did and the Scots bullocks drew the body up to the windy hilltop where the church now stands.

Port Quin

The churchyard is a forest of upright Delabole slate headstones, a rich grey-blue stone, inscribed with epitaphs—the art of engraving lettering on slate continued in this district into the present century—names and rhymes set out on the stone spaciously, letters delicate and beautiful. From the outside it's the usual Cornish church—a long low building of elvan stone, most of it built in Tudor times. But the tower is extra special. It is of huge blocks of granite brought, they say, from Lundy Island. The ground stage of the tower is strongly moulded but the builders seem to have grown tired and to have taken less trouble with the detail higher up, though the blocks of granite are still enormous.

I can remember Endellion before its present restoration. There's a photograph of what it used to look like in the porch—pitchpine pews, pitchpine pulpit, swamping with their yellow shine the clustered granite columns of the aisles. Be careful as you open the door not to fall over. Three steps *down* and there it is, long and wide and light and simple with no pitchpine anywhere except a lectern. A nave

51

and two aisles with barrel roofs carved with bosses, some of them old but most of them done twelve years ago by a local joiner, the village postman and the sculptress. The floor is slate. The walls are stone lightly plastered blueish-grey. There is no stained glass. Old oak and new oak benches, strong and firm and simple, fill, but do not crowd, the church. They do not hide the full length of these granite columns. The high altar is long and vast. At the end of the south aisle is the sculptured base of St Endelienta's shrine, in a blue-black slate called Cataclewse, a boxwood among stones. The church reveals itself at once. Though at first glance it is unmysterious, its mystery grows. It is the mystery of satisfying proportion—and no, not just that, nor yet the feeling of age, for the present church is almost wholly early Tudor, not very old as churches go, nor is the loving use of local materials all to do with it. Why does St Endellion seem to go on praying when there is no one in it? The Blessed Sacrament is not reserved here, yet the building is alive.

There is something strange and exalting about this windy Cornish hill top looking over miles of distant cliffs, that cannot be put into words.

Down a path from the north door, bordered with fuchsias, is the Rectory. The Rector of St Endellion is also a Prebendary. This church is run by a college of priests like St George's Chapel, Windsor. There are four prebends in the college, though their building is gone and they live elsewhere. They are the prebends of Marny, Trehaverock, Endellion and Bodmin. Each of the Prebendal stalls has a little income attached to it and is held by local priests. The money is given to Christian causes. For instance, the Parish of Port Isaac, formed out of St Endellion in 1913, is financed with the income of the Bodmin Prebendary. How this heavenly medieval arrangement of a college of prebendary clergymen survived the Reformation and Commonwealth and Victorian interferers is another mystery of St Endellion for which we must thank God. It was certainly saved from extinction by the late Athelstan Riley and Lord Clifden. Episcopal attacks have been made on it; but long live St Endellion, Trehaverock, Marny and Bodmin! Hold fast. *Sancta Endelienta, ora pro nobis!* ...

I take a last look at St Endellion standing on a cliff top of this Atlantic coast. The sun turns the water into moving green. In November weather, if the day is bright, the cliffs here are in shadow. The sun cannot rise high enough to strike them. The bracken is dead and brown, the grassy cliff tops vivid green; red berries glow in bushes. Ice cream cartons and cigarette packets left by summer visitors have been blown into crevices and soaked to pulp. The visitors are there for a season. Man's life on earth will last for seventy years perhaps. But this sea will go on swirling against these green and purple rocks for centuries. Long after we are dead it will rush up in waterfalls of whiteness that seem to hang half-way up the cliff face and then come pouring down with tons of ginger-beery foam. Yet compared with the age of these rocks, the sea's life is nothing. And even the age of rocks is nothing compared with the eternal life of man. And up there on the hill in St Endellion church, eternal man comes week by week in the Eucharist. That is the supreme mystery of all the mysteries of St Endellion.

Polseath, North Cornwall.

Sunday Afternoon Service
in St Enodoc Church, Cornwall

Come on! come on! This hillock hides the spire,
Now that one and now none. As winds about
The burnished path through lady's finger, thyme
And bright varieties of saxifrage,
So grows the tinny tenor faint or loud
And all things draw towards St Enodoc.

Come on! come on! and it is five to three.

Paths, unfamiliar to golfers' brogues,
Cross the eleventh fairway broadside on
And leave the fourteenth tee for thirteenth green,
Ignoring Royal and Ancient, bound for God.
    Come on! come on! no longer bare of foot,
The sole grows hot in London shoes again.
Jack Lambourne in his Sunday navy-blue
Wears tie and collar, all from Selfridge's.
There's Enid with a silly parasol,
And Graham in gray flannel with a crease
Across the middle of his coat which lay
Pressed 'neath the box of his Meccano set,
Sunday to Sunday.
            Still, Come on! come on!
The tinny tenor. Hover-flies remain
More than a moment on a ragwort bunch,
And people's passing shadows don't disturb
Red Admirals basking with their wings apart.
    A mile of sunny, empty sand away,
A mile of shallow pools and lugworm casts,
Safe, faint and surfy, laps the lowest tide.
    Even the villas have a Sunday look.

The Ransom mower's locked into the shed.
'I have a splitting headache from the sun,'
And bedroom windows flutter cheerful chintz
Where, double-aspirined, a mother sleeps;
While father in the loggia reads a book,
Large, desultory, birthday-present size,
Published with coloured plates by *Country Life*,
A Bernard Darwin on *The English Links*
Or Braid and Taylor on *The Mashie Shot*.
Come on! come on! he thinks of Monday's round—
Come on! come on! that interlocking grip!
Come on! come on! he drops into a doze—
Come on! come on! more far and far away
The children climb a final stile to church;
Electoral Roll still flapping in the porch—
Then the cool silence of St Enodoc.

My eyes, recovering in the sudden shade,
Discern the long-known little things within—
A map of France in damp above my pew,
Grey-blue of granite in the small arcade
(Late Perp: and not a Parker specimen
But roughly hewn on windy Bodmin Moor),
The modest windows palely glazed with green,
The smooth slate floor, the rounded wooden roof,
The Norman arch, the cable-moulded font—
All have a humble and West Country look.
Oh 'drastic restoration' of the guide!
Oh three-light window by a Plymouth firm!
Absurd, truncated screen! oh sticky pews!
Embroidered altar-cloth! untended lamps!
So soaked in worship you are loved too well
For that dispassionate and critic stare
That I would use beyond the parish bounds
Biking in high-banked lanes from tower to tower
On sunny, antiquarian afternoons.
    Come on! come on! a final pull. Tom Blake

Stalks over from the bell-rope to his pew
Just as he slopes about the windy cliffs
Looking for wreckage in a likely tide,
Nor gives the Holy Table glance or nod.
A rattle as red baize is drawn aside,
Miss Rhoda Poulden pulls the tremolo,
The oboe, flute and vox humana stops;
A Village Voluntary fills the air
And ceases suddenly as it began,
Save for one oboe faintly humming on,
As slow the weary clergyman subsides
Tired with his bike-ride from the parish church.
He runs his hands once, twice, across his face
'Dearly beloved . . .' and a bumble-bee
Zooms itself free into the churchyard sun
And so my thoughts this happy Sabbathtide.

    Where deep cliffs loom enormous, where cascade
Mesembryanthemum and stone-crop down,
Where the gull looks no larger than a lark
Hung midway twixt the cliff-top and the sand,
Sun-shadowed valleys roll along the sea.
Forced by the backwash, see the nearest wave
Rise to a wall of huge, translucent green
And crumble into spray along the top
Blown seaward by the land-breeze. Now she breaks
And in an arch of thunder plunges down
To burst and tumble, foam on top of foam,
Criss-crossing, baffled, sucked and shot again,
A waterfall of whiteness, down a rock,
Without a source but roller's furthest reach:
And tufts of sea-pink, high and dry for years,
Are flooded out of ledges, boulders seem
No bigger than a pebble washed about
In this tremendous tide. Oh kindly slate!
To give me shelter in this crevice dry.
These shivering stalks of bent-grass, lucky plant,
Have better chance than I to last the storm.

St. Enodoc

Oh kindly slate of these unaltered cliffs,
Firm, barren substrate of our windy fields!
Oh lichened slate in walls, they knew your worth
Who raised you up to make this House of God
What faith was his, that dim, that Cornish saint,
Small rushlight of a long-forgotten church,
Who lived with God on this unfriendly shore,
Who knew He made the Atlantic and the stones
And destined seamen here to end their lives
Dashed on a rock, rolled over in the surf,
And not one hair forgotten. Now they lie
In centuries of sand beside the church.
Less pitiable are they than the corpse
Of a large golfer, only four weeks dead,
This sunlit and sea-distant afternoon.
'Praise ye the Lord!' and in another key
The Lord's name by harmonium be praised.
'The Second Evening and the Fourteenth Psalm.'

Blisland

Church crawling is the richest of pleasures, it leads you to the remotest and quietest country, it introduces you to the history of England in stone and wood and glass which is always truer than what you read in books. It was through looking at churches that I came to believe in the reason why churches were built and why, despite neglect and contempt, innovation and business bishops, they still survive and continue to grow and prosper, especially in our industrial towns.

Of all the country churches of the West I have seen I think the church of St Protus and St Hyacinth, Blisland, in Cornwall, is the most beautiful. I was a boy when I first saw it, thirty or more years ago. I shall never forget that first visit—bicycling to the inland and unvisited parts of Cornwall from my home by the sea. The trees at home were few and thin, sliced and leaning away from the fierce Atlantic gales, the walls of the high Cornish hedges were made of slate stuffed in between with fern and stone crop and the pulpy green triangles of mesembryanthemum, sea vegetation of a windy sea coast country. On a morning after a storm, blown yellow spume from Atlantic rollers would be trembling in the wind on inland fields. Then, as huge hill followed huge hill and I sweated as I pushed my bicycle up and heart-in-mouth went swirling down into the next valley, the hedges became higher, the lanes ran down ravines, the plants seemed lusher, the thin Cornish elms seemed bigger and the slate houses and slate hedges gave place to granite ones. I was on the edge of Bodmin Moor, that sweet brown home of Celtic saints, that haunted, thrilling land so full of ghosts of ancient peoples whose hut circles, beehive dwellings and burial mounds jut out above the ling and heather. Great wooded valleys, white below the trees with wood anemones or blue with bluebells, form a border fence on this, the western side of Bodmin Moor.

Blisland: 'the tower is square and weathered and made of enormous blocks of moorland granite'

Perched on the hill above the woods stands Blisland village. It has not one ugly building in it and, which is unusual in Cornwall, the houses are round a green. Between the lichen-crusted trunks of elm and ash that grow on the green, you can see everywhere the beautiful moorland granite. It is used for windows, for chimney stacks, for walls. One old house has gable ends carved in it. They are sixteenth or seventeenth century and curl round like swiss rolls. The church is down a steep slope of graveyard, past slate headstones and it looks over the tree tops of a deep and elmy valley and away to the west where, like a silver shield, the Atlantic shines. An opening in the churchyard circle shows a fuchsia hedge and the Vicarage front door beyond. The tower is square and weathered and made of enormous blocks of this moorland granite, each block as big as a chest of drawers. When I first saw it, the tower was stuffed with moss and with plants which had rested here and there between the great stones. But lately it has been most vilely re-pointed in hard straight lines with cement. The church itself which seems to lean this way and that, throws out chapels and aisles in all directions. It hangs on the hillside, spotted with lichens which have even softened the slates of its roof. Granite forms the tracery of its windows, there is a granite holy-water stoup in the porch.

The whitewashed porch, the flapping notices, the door! That first thrill of turning the handle of the door of a church never seen before, or a church dearly loved and visited again and again like Blisland— who but the confirmed church crawler knows it?

Sir Ninian Comper, that great church architect, says that a church should bring you to your knees when first you enter it. Such a church is Blisland. For there before me as I open the door is the blue-grey granite arcade, the hardest of stones to carve. One column slopes outwards as though it was going to tumble down the hill and a carved wooden beam is fixed between it and the south wall to stop it falling. The floor is of blue slate and pale stone. Old carved benches of dark oak and a few chairs are the seating. The walls are white, the sun streams in through a clear west window and there—glory of glories!—right across the whole eastern end of the church is a richly-

Blisland: 'the walls are white, the sun streams in'

painted screen and rood loft. It is of wood. The panels at its base are red and green. Wooden columns, highly coloured and twisted like barley sugar, burst into gilded tracery and fountain out to hold a panelled loft. There are steps to reach this loft, in the wall. Our Lord and His Mother and St John who form the rood are over the centre of the screen. I look up and there is the old Cornish roof, shaped like the inside of an upturned ship, all its ribs richly carved, the carving shown up by white plaster panels. Old roofs, beautifully restored, are to be seen throughout the church. They stretch away beyond the cross irregularly and down the aisles. I venture in a little further, there through this rich screen I mark the blazing gold of the altars and the medieval-style glass, some of the earliest work of Mr Comper. In the nave is a pulpit shaped like a wineglass, in the Georgian style and encrusted with cherubs and fruit carved in wood.

The screen, the glory of the church, the golden altars, the stained glass and the pulpit are comparatively *new*, designed by F. C. Eden in 1897, who died a few years ago. He must have visualised this Cornish church as it was in medieval times. He did not do all the medieval things he might have done. He did not paint the walls with pictures of angels, saints and devils, he left the western windows clear that people might see their books; he put in a *Georgian* pulpit. He centred everything on the altar to which the screen is, as it were, a golden, red and green veil to the holiest mystery behind it.

What do dates and style matter in Blisland church? There is Norman work in it and there is fifteenth- and sixteenth-century work and there is sensitive and beautiful modern work. But chiefly it is a living church whose beauty makes you gasp, whose silent peace brings you to your knees, even if you kneel on the hard stone and slate of the floor, worn smooth by generations of worshippers.

The valley below the church was hot and warm when first I saw this granite cool interior. Valerian sprouted on the Vicarage wall. A fig tree traced its leaves against a western window. Grasshoppers and birds chirruped. St Protus and St Hyacinth, patron saints of Blisland church, pray for me! Often in a bus or train I call to mind your lovely church, the stillness of that Cornish valley and the first really beautiful work of man which my boyhood vividly remembers.

Cornish Cliffs

Those moments, tasted once and never done,
Of long surf breaking in the mid-day sun.
A far-off blow-hole booming like a gun—

The seagulls plane and circle out of sight
Below this thirsty, thrift-encrusted height,
The veined sea-campion buds burst into white

And gorse turns tawny orange, seen beside
Pale drifts of primroses cascading wide
To where the slate falls sheer into the tide.

More than in gardened Surrey, nature spills
A wealth of heather, kidney-vetch and squills
Over these long-defended Cornish hills.

A gun-emplacement of the latest war
Looks older than the hill fort built before
Saxon or Norman headed for the shore.

And in the shadowless, unclouded glare
Deep blue above us fades to whiteness where
A misty sea-line meets the wash of air.

Nut-smell of gorse and honey-smell of ling
Waft out to sea the freshness of the spring
On sunny shallows, green and whispering.

The wideness which the lark-song gives the sky
Shrinks at the clang of sea-birds sailing by
Whose notes are tuned to days when seas are high.

Near Tintagel

From today's calm, the lane's enclosing green
Leads inland to a usual Cornish scene—
Slate cottages with sycamore between,

Small fields and tellymasts and wires and poles
With, as the everlasting ocean rolls,
Two chapels built for half a hundred souls.

Chapel Amble, near Bodmin

Shags

Winter Seascape

The sea runs back against itself
   With scarcely time for breaking wave
To cannonade a slatey shelf
   And thunder under in a cave

Before the next can fully burst.
  The headwind, blowing harder still,
Smooths it to what it was at first—
   A slowly rolling water-hill.

Against the breeze the breakers haste,
   Against the tide their ridges run
And all the sea's a dappled waste
   Criss-crossing underneath the sun.

Far down the beach the ripples drag
   Blown backward, rearing from the shore,
And wailing gull and shrieking shag
   Alone can pierce the ocean roar.

Unheard, a mongrel hound gives tongue,
   Unheard are shouts of little boys:
What chance has any inland lung
   Against this multi-water noise?

Here where the cliffs alone prevail
   I stand exultant, neutral, free,
And from the cushion of the gale
   Behold a huge consoling sea.

Padstow

Some think of the farthest away places as Spitzbergen or Honolulu. But give me Padstow, though I can reach it any day from Waterloo without crossing the sea. For Padstow is in Cornwall and Cornwall is another country. And Padstow is farther away in spirit even than Land's End. It is less touristy than other fishing towns like Polperro and St Ives: less dramatic than Boscastle or Tintagel: only just not a village, for it has more than two thousand inhabitants. It is an ancient unobvious place, hidden away from the south-west gales below a hill on the sandy estuary of the River Camel. It does not look at the open sea but across the tidal water to the sand-dunes of rock and the famous St Enodoc Golf Course. There is no beach, only an oily harbour and remarkably large prawns may be netted where the town drains pour into the Camel.

Green Southern Railway engines came right into the brown and cream Great Western district of Cornwall, to reach Padstow. Launceston, Egloskerry, Otterham, Tresmeer, Camelford—and so on, down that windy single line. I know the stations by heart, the slate and granite-built waiting rooms, the oil lamps and veronica bushes, the great Delabole Quarry, the little high-hedged fields, and I know where the small-holdings grow fewer and the fields larger and browner, so that I can see the distant outline of Brown Willy and Rough Tor on Bodmin Moor. Then the train goes fast downhill through high cuttings and a wooded valley. We round a bend and there is the flat marsh of the Camel, there are the little rows of blackish-green cottages along the river at Egloshayle and we are at Wadebridge, next stop Padstow. The next five and a half miles beside the broadening Camel to Padstow, is the most beautiful train journey I know. See it on a fine evening at high tide with golden light on the low hills, the heron-haunted mud coves flooded over, the sudden thunder as we cross the bridge over Little Petherick creek, the glimpses of slate roofs and a deserted jetty among spindly Cornish elms, the wide and unexpected sight of open sea at the river mouth, the huge spread-out waste of water with brown ploughed fields

68

coming down to little cliffs where no waves break but only salt tides ripple up and ebb away. Then the utter endness of the end of the line at Padstow—260 miles of it from London. The smell of fish and seaweed, the crying of gulls and the warm, moist, west country air and valerian growing wild on slate walls.

The approach to Padstow I like most of all is the one I have made ever since I was a child. It is by ferry from the other side of the estuary. It was best in a bit of a sea with a stiff breeze against an incoming tide, puffs of white foam bursting up below the great head of distant Pentire and round the unapproachable cliffs of the rocky

Padstow Harbour, 1906

island of Newland which seems, from the ferry boat, to stand half-way between Pentire and Stepper Point at the mouth of the river. We would dip our hands in the water and pretend to feel seasick with each heave of the boat and then the town would spread out before us, its slate roofs climbing up the hillside from the wooden wharves of the harbour till they reached the old church tower and the semi-circle of wind-slashed elms which run as a dark belt right around the top of the town, as though to strap the town in more securely still against those south-west gales. Sometimes we would return on a fine, still evening, laden with the week's shopping, and see that familiar view lessen away from the ferry boat while the Padstow Bells, always well rung, would pour their music across the water, reminding me of Parson Hawker's lines—

Come to thy God in time!
Thus saith their pealing chime
Youth, Manhood, Old Age past!
Come to thy God at last!

Padstow is a fishing port and a shopping centre. There is an ice factory, an attractive Georgian Customs House, a hideous post office, an electric light company founded in 1911, and a gas works founded in 1868, this last, beside sad and peeling Public Rooms of yellow stucco dated 1840.

Vast numbers of service people pour in today from a desert that has been made in the neighbouring parishes of St Eval and St Merryn—a form of desert known as an aerodrome.

But the chief fact about modern Padstow to interest fact-maniacs, starts with a mermaid. She was combing her hair and singing in the estuary, when a Padstow youth went walking along the cliffs towards the open sea. He shot at her and in her rage she plunged down below the water and picked up a handful of sand which she threw towards Padstow, and that was the start of the Doom Bar. This bar is a bank of sand which for centuries has been slowly silting up the estuary.

In 1948 at a Town Council meeting a letter was read from a Yarmouth firm of ship owners: 'We have always been in the habit of sending our boats to Padstow, as we did last year, and we intend to do so again in 1949 during February, March and April. Like everyone else, we are concerned about the silting up of the estuary, making it extremely difficult to manoeuvre our ships in and out of port, and if action is not taken very soon we shall be unable to use the port at all, to our mutual detriment.' So there are hundreds of thousands of tons of agricultural silver sand, increasing and increasing. I can well remember how as a child I could see the hulks of ships which had been wrecked on the Doom Bar sticking up black out of the yellow sand. These are now all covered over. Who will take the sand away? And how will they do it. Miracles are always happening. In Padstow they are easier to believe in than in most places, because it is so ancient a town. So probably the port of Padstow will be saved, even if it is a Government Department that performs the miracle.

Slate-hung houses are built in a semi-circle round the harbour. Here and there the silver-blue tiled buildings are diversified by an old rose-coloured brick house and near me is a building called *The Abbey House*, with granite fifteenth-century quoins. A boy standing up in a dinghy propels her backwards across the calm, oily water by working an oar to and fro in the stern. I turn into the quiet square of the *Ship Hotel* and notice that Miss Tonkin's boot shop is no longer there, though her house with its ferns in the window and lace curtains, its lush, enclosed front and back gardens, still stands. I see that a jeweller's shop has been transformed into a souvenir haunt of tourists and new diamond-leaded panes look odd in the windows, and wooden beams, unknown in Cornwall, are fixed on to the outside walls. The main streets are, thank goodness, little altered. There's not much grand architecture in Padstow. It is all humble unobtrusive houses, three storeys high. Yet as soon as one of them is taken down, the look of the town suffers. I take one of the many narrow roads that lead up the hill. And as I reach the upper air near the church, I realise what a lot of gardens and houses there are in Padstow, though the place looks all slate from the waterside. For here one can look down at the roofs of the houses, on palms and ilex trees and bushes of hydrangeas peeping above slate walls. Narrow public passages pass right through houses under stone arches and lead past high garden walls, down steps under another house to a further street. And I begin to notice that this slate is not grey, as we are inclined to think is all Cornish slate, but a beautiful pale green, streaked here and there with reddish-brown. This is all hewn locally from the cliffs. Slate roofs grouted over with cement and then lime-washed, slate walls, slate paving stones and, as I near the churchyard gate, slate hedges as high as a house on either side of me, stuffed with ferns and penny-wort. I saw the little purple flowers of ivy-leaved toadflax on these hedges blooming as late as November last. Above these stone hedges are holly bushes and beyond the holly the circling belt of Cornish elms. A wrought-iron gate opens into the churchyard. In tree-shaded grass are slate headstones with deep-cut lettering of the eighteenth and early nineteenth centuries and cherubs with ploughboy faces, Victorian marble stones to sailors with carved anchors and cables. The parish church of St Petroc is built of a brown-grey slate and its large fifteenth-century windows are crisply carved out of that dark blue-black Cataclewse stone, a most beautiful hard stone for carving which lasts the centuries. The church is unusually large and lofty inside for a Cornish building. It was pleasantly restored in the last century. A huge monument with kneeling figures painted in reds and whites and yellows and blacks commemorates Sir Nicholas Prideaux, 1627, and leads me to Padstow's great house, Prideaux Place.

It stands on a grass clearing among elms, firs and many ilex trees, that specially west country tree, not far from the church, near the higher part of the town where late Georgian houses with ilex and palm-shaded gardens and glass-houses with geraniums and grapes in them, suggest the land agent, the doctor, retired tradesmen and old sea captains. A sign saying 'No through road' encourages me to walk through, and I come to a low castellated slate wall in a toy-fort Gothic style, with a genuine Gothic door of dark-blue Cataclewse stone let into it. Behind this, in full view of the road, is the E-shaped manor house. The eastern front looks over the road to its little-planted park and on to the distant low sand hills across the estuary. The feathery slate walls are battlemented on top. Over the entrance porch, in the wings, and in the spaces between them, are noble granite windows. Even the old lead rain-water heads are there, with the Prideaux crest

A seventeenth-century table tomb in Padstow churchyard

72

an which was buried

it is well known

extend
to their friend
right and true
as their due
brought out their day
to receive their pay
they had serud befor
for euer more
buried in this
time

Prideaux Place, Padstow. Garden Party, early 1900s

and initials on them. A large magnolia shelters in one fold of the house and a Georgian semi-circular bay is just seen on the south wing, looking across another part of the park. The inside of the house is said to be full of panelling and wood carving and plasterwork and fine furniture.

All this is Elizabethan and seventeenth-century. And the church and the houses in the town are medieval or Georgian. They seem comparatively new. What becomes apparent about Padstow is that it is even older than its oldest buildings. When the River Camel was narrower and when woods waved in the estuary which are now covered with sand, thirteen hundred years ago, St Petroc, Servant of God and son of a Welsh king, crossed the sea from Ireland in a coracle and landed at Trebetherick on the other side of the water. And then he crossed the river and founded a monastery which was known as Petrocstow—that is to say Petroc's church—which we now pronounce Padstow. Many miracles are recorded of him, tales of his kindness to animals, his long prayers standing in a stream on Bodmin moor where to this day his little beehive cell, made of turf and granite, survives. He raised the dead, cured the sick, tamed a savage, serpent-eating monster. A medieval life of St Petroc was discovered recently which ended thus:

'A woman, feeling thirsty one night, drank water out of a water-jug and swallowed a small serpent (in consequence of which) she was for many years in bad health. As no physicians benefited her, she was brought to the holy man. He made a mixture of water and earth which he gave the sick woman to drink, and immediately she had swallowed it she vomited a serpent three feet long, but dead, and the same hour she recovered her health and gave thanks to God.

'After these and many such like miracles, Blessed Petroc, continually longing for heavenly things, after afflicting his body with much rigour, full of days departed to God, on the day before the nones of June. The sacred body, therefore, worn out with fastings and vigils, is committed to the dust, and the bosom of Abraham receives his spirit, the angels singing to welcome it. At his tomb miracles frequently take place and his bones, albeit dry, retain the power of his virtues. May his glorious merits intercede for us with Christ, Who with the Father liveth and reigneth world without end. AMEN.'

I do not know whether St Petroc's day, the 4th of June, is still kept in Padstow church; it is in Bodmin parish church and in most of the other thirty or forty churches in Wales, Devon and Cornwall which are dedicated to him. His cult has survived too in Brittany and at Loperec (Locus Petroci) they have a statue of him, a more lively one than the little stone one in Padstow church. It shows a benign, bearded man in a spangled cloak, in one hand he holds the gospels and with the other he strokes a thin, nobbly little deer which has jumped up to him and put its forepaws on his breast. Blessed St

Petroc! He was the chief of all Cornish saints, a man of pervading gentleness.

St Petroc may be neglected in Padstow today. But the Hobby-horse is not. Whether it came in with the Danes who sacked the town in 981 and drove St Petroc's monks to Bodmin or whether it was a pagan rite which St Petroc himself may have witnessed with displeasure, I leave to antiquarians to dispute. The Padstow Hobby-horse is a folk revival which is almost certainly of pagan origin. Moreover, it is as genuine and unselfconscious as the Morris Dancing at Bampton-in-the-Bush, Oxfordshire, and not even broadcasting it or an influx of tourists will take the strange and secret character from the ceremonies connected with it. For this is what happens. On the day before May Day, green boughs are put up against the houses. And that night every man and woman in Padstow is awake with excitement. I knew someone who was next to a Padstow man in the trenches in the 1914 war. On the night before May Day, the Padstow man became so excited he couldn't keep still. The old 'obby 'oss was mounting in his blood and his mates had to hold him back from jumping over the top and dancing about in No-man's-land.

Now imagine a still night, the last of April, the first of May. Starlight above the chimney pots. Moon on the harbour. Moonlight shadows of houses on opposite slate walls. At about two in the morning the song begins. Here are the words.

> 'With a merry ring and with the joyful spring,
>   For summer is a-come unto day
> How happy are those little birds which so merrily do sing
>   In the merry morning of May.'

Then the men go round to the big houses of the town singing below the windows a variety of verses—

> 'Arise up Mr Brabyn I know you well afine
> You have a shilling in your purse and I wish it were in mine.'

And then on to a house where a young girl lives—

Padstow Hobby Horse, about 1920

'Arise up Miss Lobb all in your smock of silk
And all your body under as white as any milk.'

Morning light shines on the water and the green-grey houses. Out on the quay comes the Hobby-horse—it used to be taken for a drink to a pool a mile away from the town. It is a man in a weird mask, painted red and black and white, and he wears a huge hooped skirt made of black tarpaulin which he is meant to lift up, rushing at the ladies to put it over one of their heads. The skirt used to have soot in it. A man dances with the Hobby-horse carrying a club. Suddenly, at about 11.30 in the morning, there is a pause. The Hobby-horse bows down to the ground. The attendant lays his club on its head and the day song begins, a dirge-like strain.

'Oh where is St George? Oh where is he, O?
He's down in his long boat. All on the salt sea, O.'

Then up jumps the Hobby-horse, loud shriek the girls, louder sings the crowd and wilder grows the dance—

'With a merry ring and with a joyful spring
    For summer is a-come unto day
How happy are those little birds which so merrily do sing
    In the merry morning of May.'

Seaside Golf

How straight it flew, how long it flew,
    It clear'd the rutty track
And soaring, disappeared from view
    Beyond the bunker's back
A glorious, sailing, bounding drive
That made me glad I was alive.

And down the fairway, far along
    It glowed a lonely white;
I played an iron sure and strong
    And clipp'd it out of sight,
And spite of grassy banks between
I knew I'd find it on the green.

And so I did. It lay content
    Two paces from the pin;
A steady putt and then it went
    Oh, most securely in.
The very turf rejoiced to see
That quite unprecedented three.

Ah! seaweed smells from sandy caves
    And thyme and mist in whiffs,
In-coming tide, Atlantic waves
    Slapping the sunny cliffs,
Lark song and sea sounds in the air
And splendour, splendour everywhere.

The Cotton–Taylor Match, September 1929, the 18th Green and Old
Club House—St Enodoc's Golf Course, Rock

By the Ninth Green, St Enodoc

Dark of primaeval pine encircles me
With distant thunder of an angry sea
While wrack and resin scent alternately
   The air I breathe.

On slate compounded before man was made
The ocean ramparts roll their light and shade
Up to Bray Hill and, leaping to invade,
   Fall back and seethe.

A million years of unrelenting tide
Have smoothed the strata of the steep cliffside:
How long ago did rock with rock collide
   To shape these hills?

One day the mayfly's life, three weeks the cleg's,
The woodworm's four-year cycle bursts its eggs,
The flattened centipede lets loose its legs
    And stings and kills.

Hot life pulsating in this foreshore dry,
Damp life upshooting from the reed-beds high,
Under those barrows, dark against the sky,
    The Iron Age dead—

Why is it that a sunlit second sticks?
What force collects all this and seeks to fix
This fourth March morning nineteen sixty-six
    Deep in my head?

The Hon. Sec.

The flag that hung half-mast today
    Seemed animate with being
As if it knew for whom it flew
    And will no more be seeing.

He loved each corner of the links—
    The stream at the eleventh,
The grey-green bents, the pale sea-pinks,
    The prospect from the seventh;

To the ninth tee the uphill climb,
    A grass and sandy stairway,
And at the top the scent of thyme
    And long extent of fairway.

He knew how on a summer day
  The sea's deep blue grew deeper,
How evening shadows over Bray
  Made that round hill look steeper.

He knew the ocean mists that rose
  And seemed for ever staying,
When moaned the foghorn from Trevose
  And nobody was playing;

The flip of cards on winter eves,
  The whisky and the scoring,
As trees outside were stripped of leaves
  And heavy seas were roaring.

He died when early April light
  Showed red his garden sally
And under pale green spears glowed white
  His lilies of the valley:

That garden where he used to stand
  And where the robin waited
To fly and perch upon his hand
  And feed till it was sated.

The Times would never have the space
  For Ned's discreet achievements;
The public prints are not the place
  For intimate bereavements.

A gentle guest, a willing host,
  Affection deeply planted—
It's strange that those we miss the most
  Are those we take for granted.

Looe

I came to Looe by unimportant lanes. No main roads for me. I used a one-inch map. No hill was too steep, no village too remote or too full of witches. Thus I was able to taste the full flavour of the inland country behind Looe. Burnt brown August hedges were high as houses either side of narrow lanes. Grey-slated farms with granite round their windows hung on hill slopes. Little fields descended in steps of grass to deserted mines, to meadows heavy with the smell of mint.

On the hills above the lushness it is bleak indeed. Anything that dares to grow to any size is blown backwards from the sea. Ash trees and sloe bushes form a tunnel of twisted branches across the lane. Woods of oak and elm and beech belonging to mysterious country houses just peep above the hills and—phew!—the gale catches them, turns their leaves brown with salt and slices the tree-tops level with the hill.

Then, down, down, down for nearly two miles into Looe. I had a glimpse through oak trees of dark green river-water flecked with white wings of gulls. I saw overhanging woods enfolding the Looe and West Looe rivers, and in the mud the rotting hulks of ships.

Looe is two towns, East Looe and West Looe, one on each side of a steep valley. The oldest parts of the two towns are down on the waterside. Yachts, dinghies, and fishing boats are anchored in the river. There are wharves. They have old roofs of wonderful silvery-grey slate, and so have the older houses behind them. In East Looe, the bigger and more prosperous of the two old towns, the old streets are along the quay-sides. In West Looe the prettier and less-visited town, old houses climb a hill from an octagonal market house (1853), now a grocer's shop. The pavements on this hill are made of big brown pebbles; on either side of the road are white-washed cottages, black-tarred at their bases. It is quite easy to see how these two places grew, just from looking at the villages. And the best way to see them is not by road, but by water.

When I first came into Looe by road I was disappointed. I could hardly see the two old towns, and the long Victorian stone bridge which joins them—I could hardly see the houses for motor-cars. Motor coaches from Manchester, new private cars like sleek sausages (priority for Government officials), battered pre-war motors belonging to failed literary gents like me, there they stretched along the quays in thousands. Wherever there was a space in either Looe for a car park there *was* a car park. And it was full. You could hardly hear the wail of seagulls above the dance music relayed from wireless sets in the new motor-cars. Wasps gnawed at synthetic cakes in cafés. The fizzy lemonade that we drank with our fish and chips was warm. We could hardly move in the quaint old main streets of East Looe, for the thousands gazing into windows of Ye Olde Gifte Shoppes; chain stores jammed their flashy fronts into old houses. No guide books to Looe were available in any of the shops. And where, oh where was the sea? But the way to see the towns is by water.

As I put out the noise fell away. There were just the chug-chug of an outboard engine, the wail of gulls, the old and silvery wharves of Looe slipping past us as we headed up-stream for Trenant woods and those great lakes of dark green water I had seen as we entered the town. It is easy to see how the towns grew. First the ancient fishing ports either side of the water. They had their Mayors and Corporations, and sent Members to Parliament—the old rotten borough of pre-progressive days; birth-places of famous sailors, brave Elizabethans. Then a few Georgian houses were built inland, among these great enfolding woods where the two rivers divide and wind to nothingness deep in inland Cornwall. Then came the railway down the valley from Liskeard, in the wake of the new town hall and the ugly Victorian church of East Looe—the old parish church of St Martin's, a splendid building, is more than a mile away up among the hills—and the town had started to change from fishing port to watering place. We turned the boat round and slid fast with the tide back along the quays. All up the cliffs above the town were perched the boarding houses, Plymouth-style in grey cement or cream, drain pipes and bay window frames painted green, the name of the boarding house writ large on a board above the second floor windows. Most houses have a view above the old towns and out to cliffs and open sea.

Looking towards West Looe from the Banjo Pier, about 1910

And here we were sliding past the Banjo pier and the tiny sand beach behind it, and out to open sea ourselves. We went round Looe island with its three houses and woodland belt of elder bushes. We saw the sloping cliffs by Talland church. We saw the cliffs stretch east to Downderry and Rame. They are not the great rocky heights of the north coast. They are greener, earthier, more sloping cliffs—but equally impressive. Looe was out of sight behind its headlands. Only modern bungalows beyond West Looe—with those detestable red roofs which look so ugly in the slate and granite of old Cornwall— only the bungalows remind us that we are not back in the ancient marine kingdom of Cornwall.

Greenaway

I know so well this turfy mile,
    These clumps of sea-pink withered brown,
The breezy cliff, the awkward stile,
    The sandy path that takes me down

To crackling layers of broken slate
    Where black and flat sea-woodlice crawl
And isolated rock pools wait
    Wash from the highest tides of all.

I know the roughly blasted track
    That skirts a small and smelly bay
And over squelching bladderwrack
    Leads to the beach at Greenaway.

Down on the shingle safe at last
    I hear the slowly dragging roar
As mighty rollers mount to cast
    Small coal and seaweed on the shore,

And spurting far as it can reach
    The shooting surf comes hissing round
To heave a line along the beach
    Of cowries waiting to be found.

Tide after tide by night and day
    The breakers battle with the land
And rounded smooth along the bay
    The faithful rocks protecting stand.

But in a dream the other night
    I saw this coastline from the sea
And felt the breakers plunging white
    Their weight of waters over me.

There were the stile, the turf, the shore,
    The safety line of shingle beach
With every stroke I struck the more
    The backwash sucked me out of reach.

Back into what a water-world
    Of waving weed and waiting claws?
Of writhing tentacles uncurled
    To drag me to what dreadful jaws?

A ROUGH SEA ON THE CORNISH COAST.

Sunset, Cornish Coast. Julius Olsson RA

On a Painting by Julius Olsson RA

Over what bridge-fours has that luscious sea
    Shone sparkling from its frame of bronzéd gold
    Since waves of foaming opalescence roll'd
One warm spring morning, back in twenty-three,
All through the day, from breakfast-time till tea,
    When Julius Olsson, feeling rather cold,
    Packed up his easel and, contented, stroll'd
Back to St Ives, its fisher-folk and quay.

Over what bridge-parties, cloche-hat, low waist,
    Has looked that seascape, once so highly-prized,
    From Lenygon-green walls, until, despised—
'It isn't art. It's only just a knack'—
    It fell from grace. Now, in a change of taste,
See Julius Olsson slowly strolling back.

North Coast Recollections

No people on the golf-links, not a crack
Of well-swung driver from the fourteenth tee,
No sailing bounding ball across the turf
And lady's slipper of the fairway. Black
Rises Bray Hill and, Stepper-wards, the sun
Sends Bray Hill's phantom stretching to the church.
The lane, the links, the beach, the cliffs are bare
The neighbourhood is dressing for a dance
And lamps are being lit in bungalows.
    O! thymy time of evening: clover scent
And feathery tamarisk round the churchyard wall
And shrivelled sea-pinks and this foreshore pale
With silver sand and sharpened quartz and slate
And brittle twigs, bleached, salted and prepared
For kindling blue-flamed fires on winter nights.
    Here Petroc landed, here I stand today;
The same Atlantic surges roll for me
As rolled for Parson Hawker and for him,
And spent their gathering thunder on the rocks
Crashing with pebbly backwash, burst again
And strewed the nibbled fields along the cliffs.

    When low tides drain the estuary gold
Small intersecting breakers far away
Ripple about a bar of shifting sand
Where centuries ago were waving woods
Where centuries hence, there will be woods again.

    Within the bungalow of Mrs Hanks
Her daughter Phoebe now French-chalks the floor.
Norman and Gordon in their dancing pumps
Slide up and down, but can't make concrete smooth.
'My Sweet Hortense . . .'

Stepper Point from Polzeath

Sings louder down the garden than the sea.
'A practice record, Phoebe. Mummykins,
Gordon and I will do the washing-up.'
'We picnic here; we scrounge and help ourselves,'
Says Mrs Hanks, and visitors will smile
To see them all turn to it. Boys and girls
Weed in the sterile garden, mostly sand
And dead tomato-plants and chicken-runs.
Today they cleaned the dulled Benares ware
(Dulled by the sea-mist), early made the beds,
And Phoebe twirled the icing round the cake
And Gordon tinkered with the gramophone
While into an immense enamel jug
Norman poured 'Eiffel Tower' for lemonade.
  O! healthy bodies, bursting into 'teens
And bursting out of last year's summer clothes,
Fluff barking and French windows banging to
Till the asbestos walling of the place
Shakes with the life it shelters, and with all
The preparations for this evening's dance.

  Now drains the colour from the convolvulus,
The windows of Trenain are flashing fire,
Black sways the tamarisk against the West,
And bathing things are taken in from sills.
One child still zig-zags homewards up the lane,
Cold on bare feet he feels the dew-wet sand.
Behind him, from a walk along the cliff,
Come pater and the mater and the dogs.

  Four macrocarpa hide the tennis club.
Two children of a chartered actuary
(Beaworthy, Trouncer, Heppelwhite and Co.),
Harold and Bonzo Trouncer are engaged
In semi-finals for the tournament.
'Love thirty!' Pang! across the evening air
Twangs Harold's racquet. Plung! the ball returns.

Experience at Budleigh Salterton
Keeps Bonzo steady at the net. 'Well done!'
'Love forty!' Captain Mycroft, midst applause,
Pronounces for the Trouncers, to be sure
He can't be certain Bonzo didn't reach
A shade across the net, but Demon Sex,
That tulip figure in white cotton dress,
Bare legs, wide eyes and so tip-tilted nose
Quite overset him. Harold serves again
And Mrs Pardon says it's getting cold,

Rock: 'A neighbouring and less exclusive place,' June 1906

Miss Myatt shivers, Lady Lambourn thinks
These English evenings are a little damp
And dreams herself again in fair Shanghai.
'Game . . . AND! and thank you!'; so the pair from Rock
(A neighbouring and less exclusive place)
Defeated, climb into their Morris Ten.
'The final is tomorrow! Well, good night!'
    He lay in wait, he lay in wait, he did,
John Lambourn, curly-headed; dewy grass
Dampened his flannels, but he still remained.
The sunset drained the colours black and gold,
From his all-glorious First Eleven scarf.
But still he waited by the twilit hedge.
Only his eyes blazed blue with early love,
Blue blazing in the darkness of the lane,
Blue blazer, less incalculably blue,
Dark scarf, white flannels, supple body still,
First love, first light, first life. A heartbeat noise!
His heart or little feet? A snap of twigs
Dry, dead and brown the under branches part
And Bonzo scrambles by their secret way.
First love so deep, John Lambourn cannot speak,
So deep, he feels a tightening in his throat,
So tender, he could brush away the sand
Dried up in patches on her freckled legs,
Could hold her gently till the stars went down,
And if she cut herself would staunch the wound,
Yes, even with this First Eleven scarf,
And hold it there for hours.
So happy, and so deep he loves the world,
Could worship God and rocks and stones and trees,
Be nicer to his mother, kill himself
If that would make him pure enough for her.
And so at last he manages to say
'You going to the Hanks's hop tonight?'
'Well, I'm not sure. Are you?' 'I think I may—
'It's pretty dud though—only lemonade.'

Sir Gawain was a right and goodly knight
Nor ever wist he to uncurtis be.
So old, so lovely, and so very true!
Then Mrs Wilder shut the Walter Crane
And tied the tapes and tucked her youngest in
What time without amidst the lavender
At late last 'He' played Primula and Prue
With new-found liveliness, for bed was soon.
And in the garage, serious seventeen
Harvey, the eldest, hammered on, content,
Fixing a mizzen to his model boat.
'Coo-ee! Coo-ee!' across the lavender,
Across the mist of pale gypsophila
And lolling purple poppies, Mumsie called,
A splendid sunset lit the rocking-horse
And Morris pattern of the nursery walls.
'Coo-ee!' the slate-hung, goodly-builded house
And sunset-sodden garden fell to quiet.
'Prue! Primsie! Mumsie wants you. Sleepi-byes!'
Prue jumped the marigolds and hid herself,
Her sister scampered to the Wendy Hut
And Harvey, glancing at his Ingersoll,
Thought 'Damn! I must get ready for the dance.'
   So on this after-storm-lit evening
To Jim the raindrops in the tamarisk,
The fuchsia bells, the sodden matchbox lid
That checked a tiny torrent in the lane
Were magnified and shining clear with life.
Then pealing out across the estuary
The Padstow bells rang up for practice-night
An undersong to birds and dripping shrubs.
The full Atlantic at September spring
Flooded a final tide-mark up the sand,
And ocean sank to silence under bells,
And the next breaker was a lesser one
Then lesser still. Atlantic, bells and birds
Were layer on interchanging layers of sound.

Sources and Acknowledgements

Summoned by Bells was published in 1960. 'One Man's County' was broadcast on BBC Television in 1964. 'Old Friends', 'Tregardock', 'Cornish Cliffs', 'Winter Seascape', 'The Hon. Sec.' and 'By the Ninth Green, St Enodoc' were published in *High and Low*, 1966. 'Cornwall' was the Introduction to *Cornwall, A Shell Guide*, 1964. 'Delectable Duchy' and 'On a Painting by Julius Olsson RA' were published in *A Nip in the Air*, 1974. 'Saint Cadoc' and 'Trebetherick' were published in *Old Lights for New Chancels*, 1940. 'Port Isaac', 'St Endellion', 'Blisland', 'Padstow', and 'Looe' were published in *First and Last Loves*, 1952. 'Sunday Afternoon Service in St Enodoc Church, Cornwall' was published in *New Bats in Old Belfries*, 1945. 'Seaside Golf' and 'Greenaway' were published in *A Few Late Chrysanthemums*, 1954. 'North Coast Recollections' was published in *Selected Poems*, 1948.

The Publishers are grateful to the following for permission to use their photographs:
A. Fairclough, title spread; County Museum and Art Gallery, Truro, pp 11, 17, 27, 40–1, 42, 69, 74, 77, 85, 93; the late Edwin Smith (Olive Cook), pp 21, 23, 61, 64; John Gay, pp 25, 34, 58, 91; Ralph Hocking, p 12; Joe Whitlock Blundell, pp 29, 66; Alan Bartram, p 73; The Hon. Secretary, St Enodoc's Golf Club, p 78; Royal Academy of Arts, p 88; George W. F. Ellis Ltd, Bodmin, p 65; Jonathan Stedall, cover photographs.

The line drawings are by John Piper.